Simply Sewing

Written by
Judy Ann Sadler

Illustrated by
Jane Kurisu

KIDS CAN PRESS

To my parents, Frank and Rieka Bertens,
for stitching our family together with love.

Text © 2004 Judy Ann Sadler
Illustrations © 2004 Jane Kurisu

KIDS CAN DO IT and the ⬛ logo are registered trademarks of Kids Can Press Ltd.

Kids Can Press acknowledges the financial support of the Government of Ontario, through the Ontario Media Development Corporation's Ontario Book Initiative, and the Government of Canada, through the BPIDP, for our publishing activity.

Published in Canada by
Kids Can Press Ltd.
29 Birch Avenue
Toronto, ON M4V 1E2

Published in the U.S. by
Kids Can Press Ltd.
2250 Military Road
Tonawanda, NY 14150

www.kidscanpress.com

Edited by Laurie Wark
Designed by Karen Powers
Photography by Frank Baldassarra

Printed and bound in China

The hardcover edition of this book is smyth sewn casebound.
The paperback edition of this book is limp sewn with a drawn-on cover.

CM 04 0 9 8 7 6 5 4 3 2
CM PA 04 0 9 8 7 6 5 4 3 2

National Library of Canada Cataloguing in Publication Data

Sadler, Judy Ann, 1959–

Simply sewing / written by Judy Ann Sadler ; illustrated by Jane Kurisu.

(Kids can do it)

ISBN-13: 978-1-55337-659-0 (bound).   ISBN-13: 978-1-55337-660-6 (pbk.)
ISBN-10: 1-55337-659-5 (bound).   ISBN-10: 1-55337-660-9 (pbk.)

1. Sewing — Juvenile literature. I. Kurisu, Jane II. Title. III. Series.

TT712.S333 2004   j646.2   C2003-906539-1

Kids Can Press is a ℓ☺ⅠᘮS™ Entertainment company

Contents

Introduction

Imagine rolling out of bed wearing pj pants you designed and stitched together yourself, changing into a cool skirt you converted from an old pair of jeans, then tossing the stuff you need for the day into your handmade tote bag. In this book, you'll find all the information you need to hand- and machine-stitch your way through many fun projects such as these. Sew a handy makeup bag, an easy-breezy beach wrap and a cozy blanket you can stuff into a sack. Be sure to check out the And sew on … sections for other great ideas. After making the items in this book, you'll be inspired to create your own designs. Gather, borrow and buy the supplies you need and get going on sewing!

SEWING SUPPLIES

Sewing kit

You'll need a box, basket or plastic container to hold these basic sewing supplies. Keep your kit out of reach of young children and pets.

- a measuring tape
- a ruler
- a pencil
- fabric markers
- scissors
- straight pins
- different-sized sewing needles
- a pincushion (see page 14)
- a few spools of thread
- a seam ripper
- a few large and small safety pins

Scissors

Use small, sharp scissors for trimming threads and large, sharp scissors for cutting fabric. Pinking shears cut a zigzag edge to prevent fabric from fraying.

Straight pins

It's best to use straight pins with beads on the ends, called glass-head pins. They are easy to hold and to find if you drop one. Be sure to remove them as you are sewing — if a sewing machine needle hits a pin, both can break, causing mechanical problems.

Thread

Sew with good-quality, general-purpose polyester thread that matches your fabric. If you want your stitching to stand out, choose a contrasting color. You can use the same thread for hand- and machine-sewing.

Needles

For most hand sewing, use a needle called a sharp. For heavy fabrics or when sewing with embroidery floss or yarn, use a sturdy chenille needle. See page 10 for information on sewing machine needles.

Seam ripper

A seam ripper is used to remove stitches in a seam or to cut open a buttonhole. Always handle a seam ripper with care, as the blade is sharp.

Fabric markers

To mark fabrics, use a water-erasable fabric marker (the marks disappear when you dab water on them), a sharp pencil, a dressmaker's marker or a chalk pencil.

Ruler

You can use a regular 30 cm (12 in.) ruler, but it's best to have a long, see-through acrylic quilter's ruler. It makes marking fabric easy because it has many different lines printed on it and you can see the fabric's edge through the ruler.

Iron

Whenever the instructions tell you to iron, ask an adult to help you. Iron on a sturdy ironing board with a padded cover. Test the temperature of your iron on fabric scraps first to make sure it's not too hot. Don't iron synthetic fleece, such as Polarfleece or Arctic fleece, because it may melt.

MEASURING

Measurements are given in both metric and imperial. Choose one measurement system and use it for the entire project.

Fabric

The instructions for each project in this book give guidelines for what types of fabric to use. You may already have the fabric you need at home, or check the remnant bins at fabric stores for inexpensive pieces. It's also fun to choose the perfect fabric right off the bolt. Fabric is sold in meters and yards or in smaller amounts. If you like, buy extra fabric to swap with friends. When you buy fabric, ask how it should be laundered. Most cotton fabrics should be washed and ironed before sewing so that your finished item doesn't shrink when it's washed. Used-clothing stores are a great place to buy inexpensive jeans, T-shirts and cardigans to use for projects.

Fabric sides

When the instructions refer to the right side of the fabric, this means the good side, the patterned side or the side that shows on your finished project. The wrong side often looks faded and is usually on the inside where it cannot be seen. Some fabrics are the same on both sides.

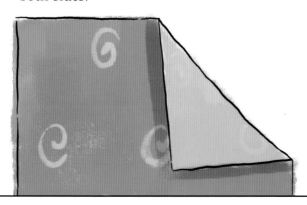

Cutting fabric

Before you use your fabric, it's important to make sure that the edges are straight. Some fabrics can be torn straight by making a small cut at an edge and then tearing straight across the width. Other fabrics can be cut straight along their stripes or regular patterns. You can also try pulling fabric from corner to corner to straighten it. Once your fabric is straightened, measure and mark it carefully, then cut or tear it to the proper measurements.

Fabric edges

Raw edges refer to fabric edges that have been cut or torn and are not yet finished with a hem, zigzag stitch or pinking shears. They will fray if left raw. Selvage edges are factory made and do not fray. A new piece of fabric will have two raw edges and two selvage edges.

Hand-sewing basics

Most of the projects in this book can be sewn by hand if you don't have a sewing machine; it will just take more time. Refer to these pages whenever you need hand-sewing information.

Threading a needle

Cut a 50 cm (20 in.) length of thread. Wet one end in your mouth, pinch it together and thread it through the eye of the needle. Or use a needle threader by poking the wire loop through the eye of the needle, dropping the thread through the loop, then pulling the wire and threading it back through the eye.

Knotting the thread

To make a knot, wet your index finger and wind the longer thread end around it once. (If the instructions call for doubled thread, make the ends even, then wind both ends around your index finger.) With your thumb, roll the thread off your finger and pull down to make a knot.

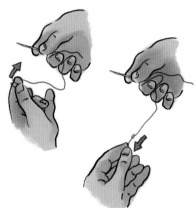

Ending the stitching

When you run out of thread or reach the end of your stitching, make two or three small stitches over or near the last stitch. Make a small loop on the wrong side of the fabric and bring your needle through it. With the tip of your needle, hold the loop close to the fabric, then tighten the knot. Trim the leftover thread.

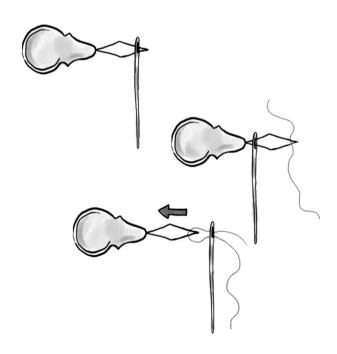

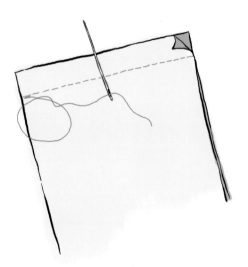

Hand-sewing stitches

Backstitch

If you don't have a sewing machine, this is the stitch you will use to sew fabric together.

1. With knotted thread in your needle, push the needle up through the fabric about 0.5 cm (¼ in.) in from where you want the stitch line to start.

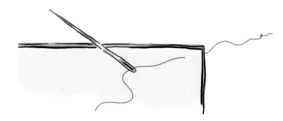

2. Make a small stitch backward, then push the needle up through the fabric a little way in front of the first stitch.

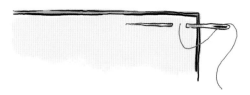

3. Push the needle down through the fabric where it first came up. Keep stitching in this way, making the stitches small and even.

Overcast stitch

You can use the overcast stitch instead of the machine zigzag stitch (page 12) along your fabric's raw edges.

1. With knotted thread in your needle, push the needle up through the fabric.

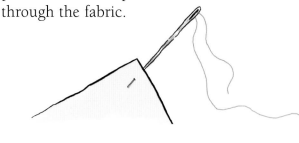

2. Bring the needle around the edge of the fabric and push it up through the fabric a little way along from the first stitch. Keep stitching in this way.

Buttonhole stitch

If your sewing machine doesn't have a buttonhole stitch, here's how to make one by hand. The buttonhole should be the length of your button or the length given in the project instructions.

1. Cut a slit with scissors or a seam ripper where you want your buttonhole to be. Trim any threads that unravel from the slit.

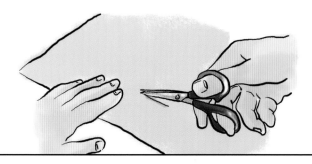

2. With the right side facing you, hold the fabric so the slit is horizontal.

3. With knotted thread in your needle, push the needle up through the fabric on the left end just above the slit.

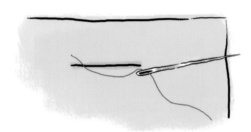

4. Insert the needle right beside where it just came up, but poke its tip partway through the slit. Wrap the thread around the tip of the needle and pull the needle the rest of the way through the fabric. Keep stitching in this way, making the stitches small and close together.

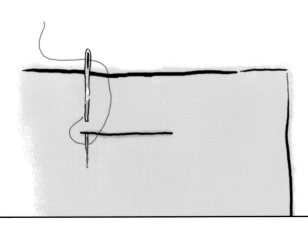

Sewing on buttons

For flat and shank buttons, double the thread in your needle by pulling the ends even and knotting them together at the ends.

1. Push the tip of the needle up through the fabric where the button will be stitched.

2. Pull the needle up through one hole of a flat button and down through the hole beside it. Whether the button has two or four holes, sew each pair of holes five or six times. Four-hole buttons can also be stitched on in an **X** or square design.

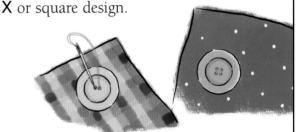

For a shank button, pull the needle through the button shank and back into the fabric close beside where your needle just came up. Keep stitching this way five or six times.

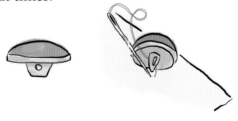

3. Make a couple of small stitches on the wrong side of the fabric, knot the thread and trim it.

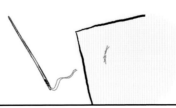

Sewing-machine basics

There are many different types of sewing machines, from very simple ones to computerized machines with fancy stitches and automatic features. For the projects in this book, you'll need a sewing machine with straight, reverse, zigzag and basting stitches, and it's also helpful to have a buttonhole stitch. Have someone show you how to thread the machine, wind the bobbin, adjust the stitches, change the feet and tell you about its features. You can also check the owner's manual for this information. Here are some basics to get you started.

Needle

Check your sewing machine manual for the types of needles you need and how to change them. Generally, you will need a slender needle for fine fabrics and a heavy one for thick fabrics. Sewing machine needles become dull after a few projects, so change them regularly.

Bobbin

The bobbin holds the lower thread, which loops around the top thread to form stitches in your fabric. The bobbin is held in a bobbin case below the needle. It should be wound with the same thread you are using in your needle.

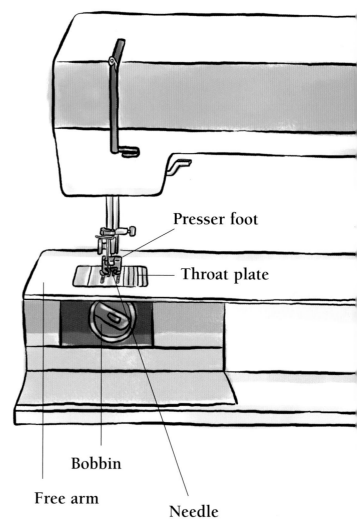

Presser foot

Throat plate

Bobbin

Free arm

Needle

Hand wheel

Foot pedal

Presser foot

The presser foot holds your fabric in place as you are sewing. It is controlled by a lever and is always in the lowered position when your machine is in use. You will use the general-purpose foot for most sewing. Use the zipper foot for sewing in zippers and a buttonhole foot for making buttonholes.

Throat plate

This metal plate below the presser foot covers the bobbin case. It has openings for the teeth that guide your fabric and for the needle to meet the bobbin thread. On some machines, part of the throat plate slides open so you can put in the bobbin. The throat plate usually has measurements marked on it to use as a guide as you are sewing. If it doesn't, you can mark them with masking tape.

Flat bed and free arm

The flat bed is the table area around the free arm that supports the fabric as you are sewing. When it is removed, you are left with the free arm, which allows you to stitch around narrow openings, such as sleeves and the hems of pants.

Foot pedal

When the sewing machine power is turned on, the foot pedal acts like a gas pedal in a car, allowing you to go slowly or quickly and stop. Some machines have a knee control instead.

Hand wheel

This is the large wheel at the side of your machine. It turns as the machine stitches, but you can also work it by hand by turning it towards you. This allows you to stitch very slowly over extra-thick areas of fabric or difficult spots. Do not turn the wheel away from you.

Machine stitches

Straight stitch

This is the stitch used most often. You can adjust the length of the stitches, but usually you will use a stitch length of about 5 stitches per cm (12 stitches per in.). Practice stitching straight on fabric scraps. Use a contrasting color of thread so you can see your stitches clearly.

Reverse stitch

Sewing machines have a button or lever that you push and hold to stitch backwards. Use the reverse stitch for a few stitches at the beginning and end of every seam to keep the seam from coming undone.

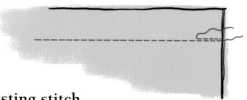

Basting stitch

Basting is used when you need to hold fabric pieces together temporarily but don't want pins in the way. Set your stitch length so that the stitches are longer than regular straight stitches. This makes it easy to remove them later. Do not reverse-stitch with basting.

Zigzag stitch

This stitch is used mainly on seams and fabric edges to prevent them from fraying. As the needle zigzags back and forth, it should be positioned so that it dips into the fabric on the left-hand side and just over the edge of the fabric on the right-hand side.

For appliqué, adjust the stitch length so that the zigzags are narrow and close together.

Seam allowance

A seam allowance is the space between the edge of the fabric and the stitching line. Use a 1.5 cm (5/8 in.) seam allowance for clothing and 1 cm (1/2 in.) or 0.5 cm (1/4 in.) for other projects. These distances are often marked on the throat plate (page 11) of your machine.

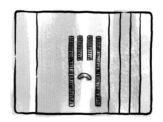

Sewing a seam

1. To begin a seam, line up your pinned fabric along the proper seam allowance underneath the presser foot about 0.5 cm (¼ in.) from the end of the seam line.

2. Lower the foot and turn the hand wheel towards you so that the needle is in the fabric. Hold the thread ends away from you for the first few stitches as you slowly press the foot pedal. Reverse-stitch for a few stitches, then continue forward gently guiding, but not pulling, the fabric through the machine.

3. Follow the marked lines on your throat plate to keep the seam straight. When you get to a pin, stop, remove it and continue.

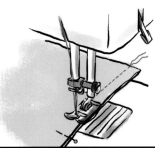

4. When you are 0.5 cm (¼ in.) from the end of the seam, stop, reverse-stitch and go forward to the end of the fabric.

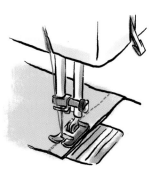

5. Use the hand wheel to bring the needle out of the fabric and up to its highest point, then stop just as it's about to start down again. Lift the presser foot and trim the threads at both ends of the seam.

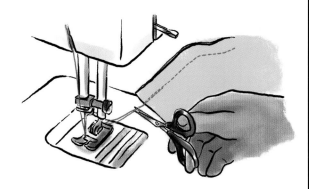

Tension

The tension on your sewing machine is set correctly if the stitches on the top and underside of the seam look even and smooth. If your seam is puckered or the stitches are loopy, the tension may not be set correctly. (You should also double-check to make sure you have the machine properly threaded.) Check your manual to learn how to adjust the tension.

Patchwork pincushion

Sort through your fabrics to find a few small pieces you especially like, then stitch together this scrappy little cushion. It will be a great addition to your sewing kit!

YOU WILL NEED

- one 10 cm (4 in.) square and one 6 cm (2¼ in.) square of thin cardboard
- five fabric scraps
- polyester fiber stuffing
- your sewing kit (page 4)

1 With a fabric marker, trace the small cardboard square onto four of the different fabric scraps. Trace the large square onto the fifth fabric. Cut out all five squares. Set aside the large one.

2 With the right sides together, pin two small squares, then straight-stitch (page 12) or backstitch (page 8) them using a 0.5 cm (¼ in.) seam allowance (page 12). Remove the pins as you sew. Stitch the other two small squares together in the same way.

3 Iron (page 5) the seams open.

4 Pin and stitch the two sewn strips so that the right sides are together and the center seams line up. Remove the pins as you sew. Iron the seam open.

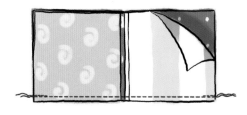

5 With the right sides together, pin the patchwork square to the large one. Begin sewing a seam (page 13) about 2 cm (3/4 in.) from one of the corners. When you are 0.5 cm (1/4 in.) from the corner, use the hand wheel (page 11) to position the needle in the fabric. Lift the presser foot, pivot the fabric, lower the foot and keep sewing this way until you are just past the fourth corner. Reverse-stitch, cut the thread and remove the fabric from the machine.

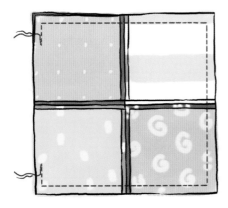

6 Make sure all the pins have been removed, then turn the fabric right side out. Stuff it. Tuck in the seam allowance and overcast-stitch (page 8) the opening closed.

And sew on ...

Make a round or heart-shaped pincushion by tracing or drawing a circle or heart onto the wrong side of the large square. Pin it to the patchwork square and stitch along your tracing line. Leave an opening for the stuffing. Trim the extra fabric, turn the fabric right side out, stuff the cushion and overcast-stitch the opening closed.

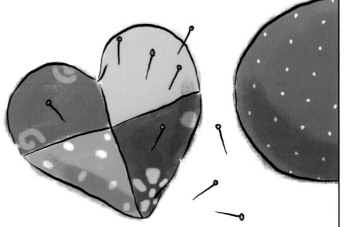

Make a large cushion or chair pad by cutting out four 20 cm (8 in.) fabric squares. Follow steps 2 to 4 except use a 1 cm (1/2 in.) seam allowance. For the cushion back, make another patchwork square the same size or cut a 38 cm (15 in.) fabric square. If you'd like to put a zipper in your pillow, see Zippy pillow (page 32). Otherwise, with the right sides together, pin, then stitch the sides, leaving an opening. Turn the fabric right side out, stuff the cushion with polyester fiberfill or a 35 cm (14 in.) pillow form. Overcast-stitch the opening closed.

Slumber sack

Sew up some pj pants (page 40) and a makeup bag (page 36), tuck them into this super-simple slumber sack along with a magazine and movie, and you'll be ready for the next sleepover party! Be sure to check out the matching cozy blanket on page 18, too!

YOU WILL NEED

- a piece of synthetic fleece about 100 cm x 33 cm (39 in. x 13 in.)
- 2 strips of fleece in a contrasting color or pattern, each about 2.5 cm x 75 cm (1 in. x 30 in.)
- your sewing kit (page 4)

1 On both short ends of the large fleece piece, fold over and pin 2.5 cm (1 in.) to form a drawstring casing. (If your fleece has a right and wrong side, fold to the wrong side.) Stitch close to the cut edge at each end. Remove the pins as you sew.

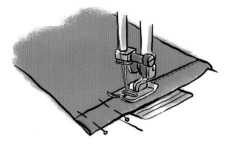

2 Fold and pin the fleece in half so that the right sides are together and even.

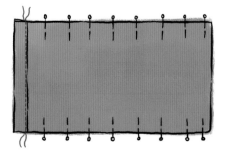

3 Using a 1 cm (½ in.) seam allowance, stitch each side seam from just below the casing to the fold. Remove the pins as you sew.

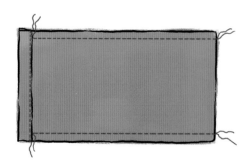

4 Turn the sack right side out.

5 Fasten a safety pin to the end of one of the strips of fleece. Beginning and ending at the left side, thread the fleece through both halves of the casing. Remove the safety pin and tie the ends together with an overhand knot.

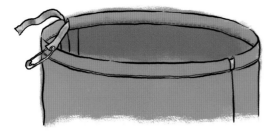

6 Safety-pin and thread the other fleece strip through the casing, beginning and ending at the right side. Remove the pin and tie the ends together with an overhand knot.

7 Pull the ties in opposite directions so that the sack closes. Strips of fleece sometimes stretch, so pull firmly on the ties, then fully open the bag. If the ties hang down, knot the ties closer to the sides of the bag and trim the extra length.

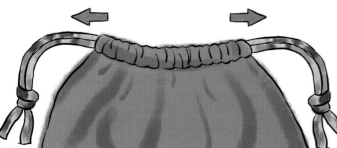

And sew on ...

🔘 Decorate the sack after step 1. See pages 46 to 48 for patterns or draw your own shape onto the same fleece you used to make the drawstrings. Cut out your shape and pin it in place on the bag. Baste (page 12) the edges. Remove the pins as you sew. Zigzag- (page 12) or blanket-stitch (page 19) around the edges. Remove the basting thread.

Roll-and-go blanket

Roll up this blanket and fit it into the Slumber sack (page 16) so it's ready to take with you to camp, a sleepover or a car trip. Together they make a great neckroll pillow, too!

YOU WILL NEED

- a 150 cm (60 in.) square of fleece
- your sewing kit (page 4)

1 Cut off any ragged or crooked edges from the fleece.

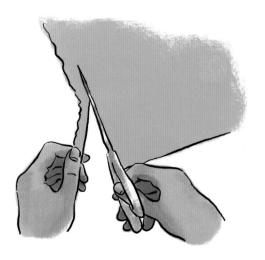

2 Fold over and pin 1 cm (½ in.) to the wrong side of the fleece along one edge only. Pin to 5 cm (2 in.) from the corner.

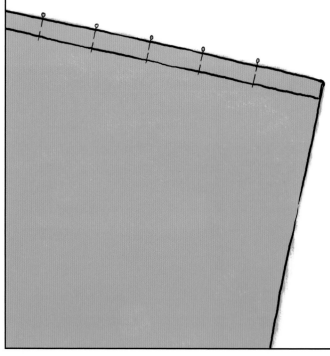

3 Stitch slowly along the inside edge, guiding the blanket under the presser foot without stretching the fleece. Remove the pins as you sew. At 5 cm (2 in.) from the corner, fold over the next edge of the fleece, refold the edge you are stitching and continue to the corner.

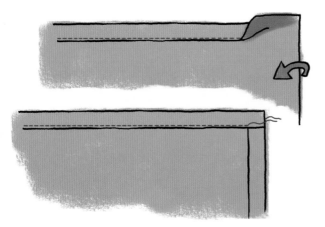

4 At the corner, use the hand wheel (page 11) to position the needle in the fleece, lift the presser foot, pivot and lower the foot. Fold and pin this edge to 5 cm (2 in.) from the next corner.

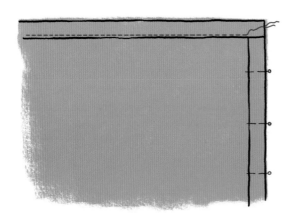

5 Repeat steps 2 to 4 until you have sewn all four edges.

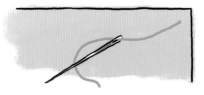

And sew on ...

See *And sew on ...* (page 17) for how to appliqué designs onto your blanket.

Blanket-stitch the edges (as shown below) using a large needle and embroidery floss or yarn.

1. With knotted embroidery floss in your needle, push the needle up through the fabric.

2. Push the needle back down about 1 cm (½ in.) from where it came up. Loop the floss behind the needle as you pull it through the fabric. This first stitch will be slanted.

3. Push the needle back down through the fabric. Keep stitching in this way.

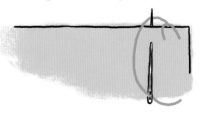

4. When you get back to where you started, push the needle under the first stitch loop, then straighten and anchor it with a tiny stitch at the edge of the fabric.

Tiny T-shirt skirt

Here's a terrific way to turn a T-shirt or jersey into a sassy little skirt or bathing suit cover-up. The more interesting the shirt, the better the skirt. The T-shirt you use must be big enough to easily go over your hips — the roomier it is, the more swing your T-shirt skirt will have!

YOU WILL NEED

- an adult-sized T-shirt
- a long ruler (optional)
- elastic 1 to 2 cm ($\frac{1}{2}$ to $\frac{3}{4}$ in.) wide (see step 7 for length)
- about 120 cm (47 in.) of cord
- your sewing kit (page 4)

1 Fold the shirt under the arms and hold it up to your waist. Adjust the fold until the shirt is 2.5 to 5 cm (1 to 2 in.) longer than you want your finished skirt to be. (If it is too short, find a longer shirt.) Draw a line along the fold. (If there is a pocket in this area, use your seam ripper to carefully remove it.)

2 Make sure the bottom of the skirt is even, then cut along your marked line through both layers of fabric.

3 For the casing, fold over 1 cm (½ in.) to the wrong side around the cut edge and iron (page 5) it. Next, fold over an additional 3 cm (1¼ in.) and iron it.

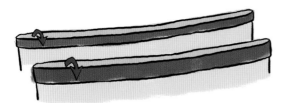

4 For the buttonholes, unfold the center and mark a 1.5 cm (⅝ in.) vertical line on each side of the center-front casing area 5 cm (2 in.) down from the cut edge.

5 To use your machine buttonhole stitch, change the foot on your machine and stitch a buttonhole on each marked line through only one layer of fabric. Carefully cut each buttonhole open with scissors or a seam ripper. Change back to the regular presser foot. To make buttonholes by hand, cut a slit through one layer of fabric on each marked line. Finish the raw edges with the buttonhole stitch (page 8).

6 Refold, pin and stitch the casing, being careful to not stretch the fabric. Remove the pins as you sew.

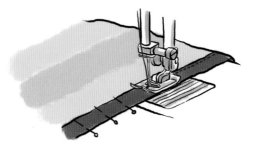

7 For the drawstring, measure your waist and divide the measurement in half. Cut a piece of the elastic this length. Zigzag-stitch each cut end of your elastic. If this is difficult on your machine, overcast-stitch (page 8) it by hand.

8 Cut the cord in half and stitch one half to each end of the elastic.

9 Fasten a safety pin to one end of the cord. Thread the drawstring into the casing through one buttonhole and out the other so that the elastic is in the center-back area. Remove the safety pin. (If the cord ends fray, dab them with clear nail polish or white craft glue.)

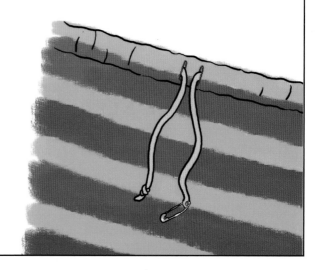

Decorating your duds

Jazz up your clothes by sewing on trims such as rickrack, braided cord, beaded fringe, mini pompoms, ribbon and buttons.

YOU WILL NEED

- a pair of jeans, pants, capris, shorts or a skirt
- assorted trims and buttons (see step 1)
- your sewing kit (page 4)

1 To figure out how much trim you will need for each row, use a measuring tape to measure around the hems of your pants and add 2.5 cm (1 in.) for overlap. If you are going to arrange the trim in a wavy or zigzag pattern, lay out the tape in the pattern you want and add 2.5 cm (1 in.).

2 Starting at the inside seam, pin on a trim. (For a skirt, start the trim at the side.) If the hemline has a slit, you can fold the trim ends to the inside of the slit at the beginning and the end of each row.

Some trims, such as piping, pompoms and beaded fringe, have a band attached to them. Pin the band to the underside of the hem so only the trim shows below the hemline. Sew the band along the existing stitching or cover the stitching line later with more trim.

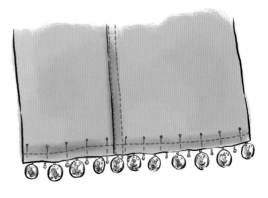

3 When you are back to where you started pinning, allow an extra 2.5 cm (1 in.) for overlap with the beginning of the trim, but don't pin the end down.

4 With thread to match the trim, start sewing at the beginning of the pinned trim. If the trim is wide, use two rows of stitches — one on each edge of the trim. If the trim is narrow, stitch down the center. Remove the pins as you sew.

Note: *When you are stitching on trims with a sewing machine, it's best to use your machine's free arm (page 11).*

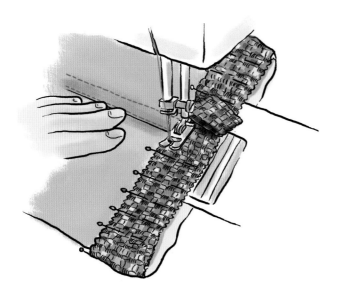

5 Stop stitching about 3 cm (1¼ in.) from the end. Fold under 1 cm (½ in.) of the trim and overlap it on the beginning of the trim.

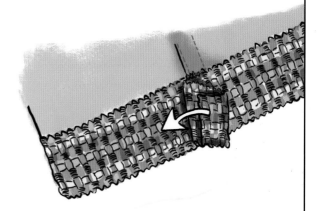

6 Repeat steps 2 to 5 to sew on the remaining trims. If you like, stitch on buttons, too (page 9).

And sew on …

🔘 You can also sew trim onto a fabric hat, pajamas, a T-shirt, and the collar, cuffs and other areas of a jacket or button-up shirt.

Jeans-to-skirt

When your favorite jeans become too short or worn at the knees, transform them into this great skirt. If you don't have extra jeans, pick up a pair from a used-clothing store.

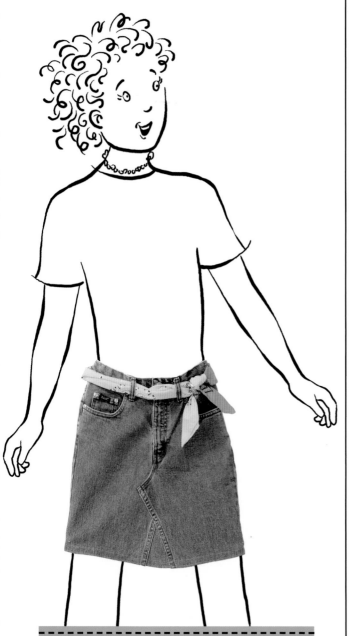

1 Try on the jeans and decide how long to make your skirt. Add 2.5 cm (1 in.) to the length, mark it, take off your jeans and cut off the legs where marked. Don't worry about cutting them perfectly straight — you can adjust them when you sew the hem.

2 Use a seam ripper to open the inside leg seams up to the crotch. Open the seam in the front up to the fly and up the back to the end of the curve, about even with the bottom of the pockets. Remove the bits of stitching thread and trim any frayed threads.

3 Lay the skirt flat and place the cardboard between the layers. Pin down the overlapping flap at the front, flip the skirt over and pin the flap at the back. Leave the edges of the flaps folded over so that no raw edges are showing. Remove the cardboard.

4 Using thread to match either the fabric or the stitching on the skirt, stitch along the remaining seam lines from the stitching you ripped out. Remove the pins as you sew.

5 On the inside, cut away the flaps that are hanging loose, but leave about 2 cm (¾ in.) of extra fabric so that you can zigzag-stitch (page 12) the edges.

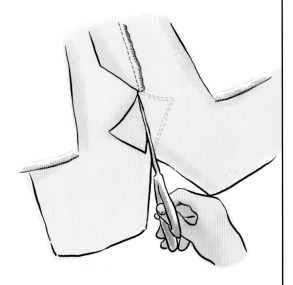

6 Open the seam on one of the cut-off legs. Cut off two pieces, each one larger than what you'll need to patch the open triangles on the front and back of the skirt.

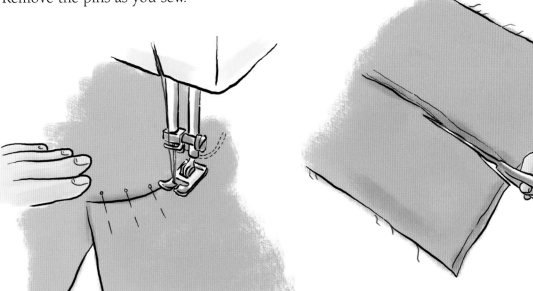

Instructions continue on the next page ☞

7 With the cardboard between the layers of the skirt, pin a patch under the triangle in the front of the skirt. Remove the cardboard, then stitch along the existing lines. (If there are no lines to follow, stitch close to the edge of the opening and again a little farther away.) Remove the pins as you sew. Patch the back in the same way.

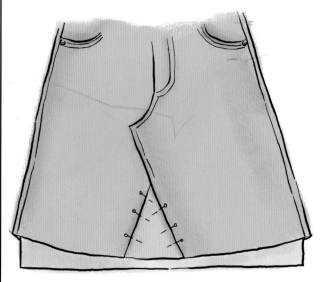

8 Turn the skirt inside out. Leaving about 2 cm (3⁄4 in.) along the edges, trim away the extra fabric around each patch. Zigzag-stitch the leftover edges.

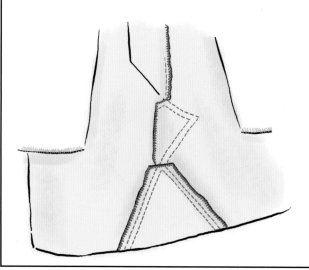

9 Try on the skirt to see if you like the length (remember that it will be shorter when you finish the hem) and to see if the hemline is straight. It may be helpful to have someone measure from the floor up to the skirt length you want and mark it. Zigzag-stitch the hemline.

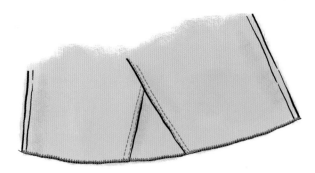

Fold it over, then iron, pin and hem it with one or two rows of stitches.

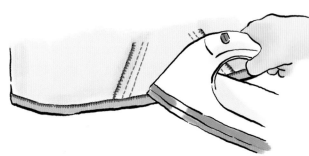

It will be tricky to sew through the double seam areas, so go slowly. Remove the pins as you sew.

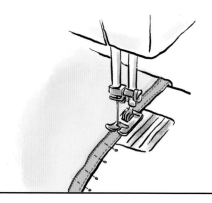

And sew on ...

⊙ Rather than patching the front and back of your skirt with denim, use an entirely different fabric or a doubled bandanna.

⊙ See page 22 for how to jazz up your jean skirt with beaded trim, rickrack and other great trims.

⊙ See page 44 for how to appliqué designs onto your new skirt.

⊙ Make a long skirt. You'll need a second pair of jeans or other fabric to fill in the triangular areas on the front and back.

⊙ Stitch up a matching denim bag. Cut off the legs just above the crotch. Turn the pants inside out, stitch the legs closed, and zigzag-stitch the seam. Turn the bag right side out. For a closure and handles, weave cord through the belt loops. Or you can stitch in Velcro at the waist. Stitch cord handles onto the sides or tie them into the belt loops.

Beach wrap

You can make this easy-breezy wrap skirt in any length. Use a lightweight fabric such as polyester or rayon.

YOU WILL NEED

- fabric, see step 1
- your sewing kit (page 4)

1 A beach wrap usually sits at the hips, so measure around yourself a little below your waist. For your fabric width, double this measurement. Now measure from below your waist to the length you'd like your skirt to be. Add 8 cm (3 in.) to this measurement. You will also need a little extra fabric for the skirt ties.

2 Cut or tear the fabric to your measurements. If you need to stitch together a couple of pieces of fabric to get the proper width, put the right sides together, then pin and stitch them, removing the pins as you sew. Iron (page 5) the seam open and zigzag-stitch the edges (page 12).

3 With wrong sides together, fold over and iron 1 cm (½ in.) and then an additional 1 cm (½ in.) along both side edges of your fabric. Pin then stitch close to the inside edge. Remove the pins as you sew.

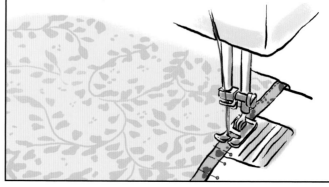

4 To make a casing, fold over 1 cm (½ in.) to the wrong side along the top edge of your skirt and iron it. Fold over, iron and pin an additional 2 cm (¾ in.) along the top edge. Stitch close to the inside edge. Remove the pins as you sew.

5 Cut two ties 3 cm x 100 cm (1¼ in. x 39 in.) from your leftover fabric.

6 Fold over and iron, to the wrong side, 0.5 cm (¼ in.) along the sides and one end of the ties.

7 Iron each tie in half along its length. Stitch each tie close to the doubled edge.

8 Tuck the raw edge of one of the ties into one end of the casing. Stitch it in place, making sure you reverse-stitch a few times. Stitch the other tie in the other end of the casing.

9 With wrong sides together, fold over and iron 1 cm (½ in.) and then an additional 1 cm (½ in.) around the hemline. Pin then stitch close to the inside edge. Remove the pins as you sew.

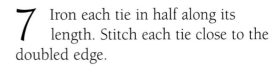

Beach bag

This sturdy tote is perfect for the beach, dance class, school or camp. If you want to appliqué (page 44) the fabric, do it before you begin the bag.

YOU WILL NEED

- two 70 cm x 10 cm (28 in. x 4 in.) strips of the sturdy fabric

- a rectangle of sturdy fabric about 100 cm x 50 cm (39 in. x 20 in.)

- your sewing kit (page 4)

1 With the wrong sides together, fold over and iron (page 5) the long edges of each shoulder strap strip so that the raw edges meet in the center. Fold and iron them again so that the newly folded edges are together.

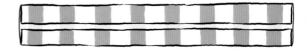

2 Pin and stitch the straps along each long edge. Remove the pins as you sew.

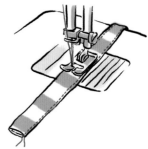

3 With the right sides together, fold the fabric for the bag in half so that the short ends are even. Pin and stitch the side seams using a 1 cm ($\frac{1}{2}$ in.) seam allowance. Remove the pins as you sew.

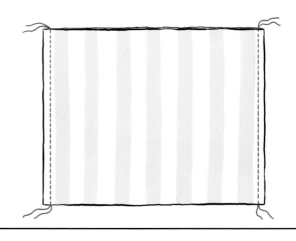

4 Zigzag-stitch (page 12) the side seam allowances together on each side.

5 With the wrong sides together, fold over and iron 1 cm (½ in.) and then an additional 3 cm (1 ¼ in.) around the top of the bag.

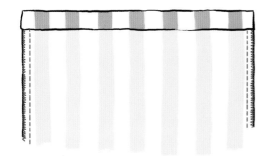

6 Measure and mark a line 15 cm (6 in.) from each side seam of the bag, front and back. Tuck a strap end under the ironed hem at each marked line. Pin the straps in place (they should be hanging upside down). Make sure they're not twisted. Pin the rest of the hem.

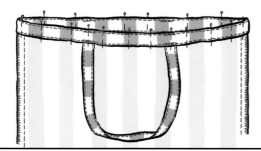

7 Stitch around the hem twice — once close to the outside edge and once close to the inside edge. Whenever you sew over one of the four strap ends, sew back and forth a couple of times. Remove the pins as you sew.

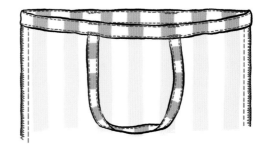

8 Flip the handles up. Sewing slowly because you are stitching through many layers, stitch back and forth across them a few times.

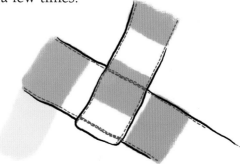

9 With the bag still inside out, iron the sides and bottom. Fold up about 8 cm (3 in.) at the bottom of the bag. Pin then stitch the fold at least twice at each side seam. Remove the pins as you sew. Turn the bag right side out.

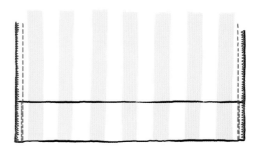

Zippy pillow

Having a zipper means that you can remove the pillow cover to wash it whenever necessary. To make different-sized pillows, cut the cover fabric 2.5 cm (1 in.) larger than your pillow form and use a zipper 5 cm (2 in.) shorter than the form.

1 Zigzag-stitch (page 12) all four sides of each fabric square.

2 With the right sides together, pin the two squares of fabric along one edge. On one square, mark lines 4 cm (1 1/2 in.) from the top and 4 cm (1 1/2 in.) from the bottom along the 1.5 cm (5/8 in.) seam line. Stitch from the top and bottom edges to the marked lines.

3 Baste (page 12) the rest of the seam between the marked area. Remove the pins as you sew. Iron (page 5) the seam open, then refold the fabric with the right sides together.

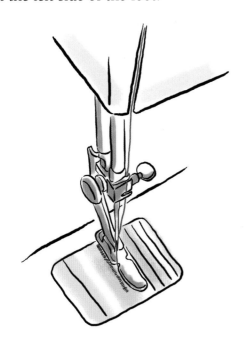

4 Replace the regular presser foot on your sewing machine with the zipper foot (check your sewing machine manual for details). The needle should be on the left side of the foot.

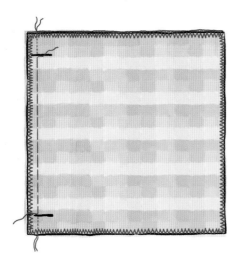

5 Place the fabric so that the seam allowance is to the right side of the fabric as shown.

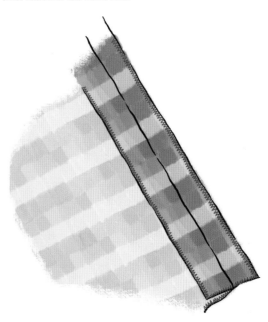

6 Unzip the zipper. Center and pin the right half face down along the seam allowance so that the teeth are resting along the seam line.

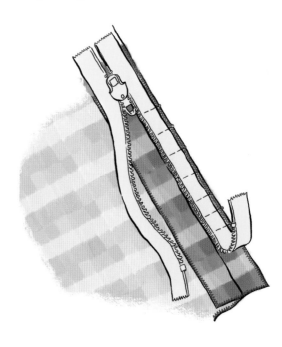

Instructions continue on the next page ☞

7 Stitch close to the teeth from the pull end of the zipper tape to the other end. The pull may be a bit tricky to get around, but try to keep your stitching straight. You will be stitching through the zipper and seam allowance only. Remove the pins as you sew.

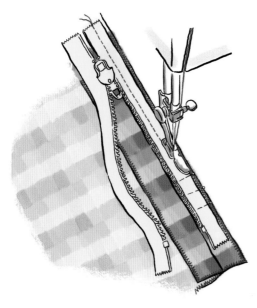

8 Change the needle or foot position so that the needle is now on the right side of the zipper foot.

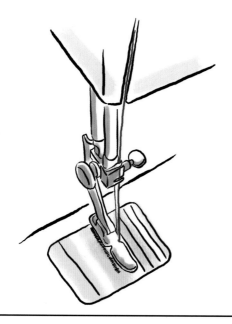

9 Zip up the zipper and turn it over so it is face up. The zipper should be on the right side and the pillow cover on the left. You'll be stitching on the narrow strip of seam allowance to the left of the zipper. Gently pull the zipper and fabric apart as you stitch up to the pull end.

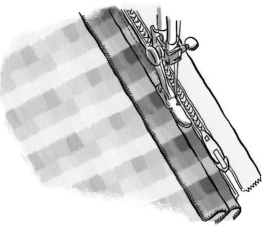

10 Open the pillow cover and lay it wrong side up with the zipper face down. Slowly stitch across the end of the zipper from the seam to just beyond the stopper. Gently pull the fabric in opposite directions to keep it smooth. Pivot and stitch the rest of the zipper fairly close to the teeth. (Again, it may be difficult to get past the zipper pull, so push it aside a little and try to keep your stitches straight.) Pivot and stitch across the top to the seam.

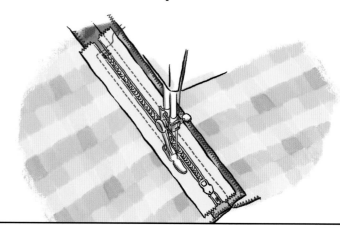

11 On the front of the pillow, use your seam ripper to remove the basting. The areas at each end of the zipper should still be stitched. Leave the zipper open.

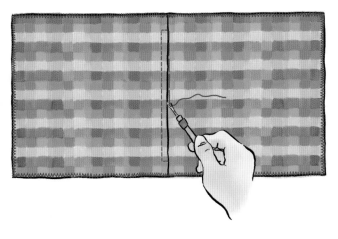

12 Change back to your machine's regular presser foot. With the right sides together, pin and stitch the remaining three sides of the pillow using a 1 cm (1/2 in.) seam allowance. Remove the pins as you sew. Turn the pillow right side out, and zip in the form.

And sew on …

Before you put in the zipper, appliqué designs (page 44) or stitch ribbon, lace, rickrack or other trim (page 22) onto the fabric.

Make an unusual pillow by cutting two squares from the front and back of an old button-up blouse, vest or cardigan. With the right sides together, stitch them on all four sides, then open the button closures, turn it right side out and stuff a pillow form inside. Button up!

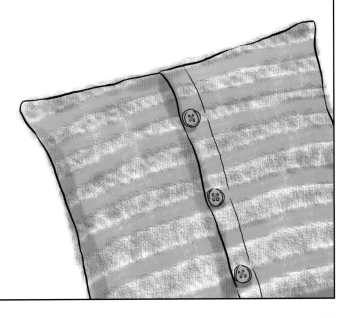

Makeup bag

After you've made this handy bag, make another one for jewelry, school supplies or extra sewing notions such as buttons, zippers and trims. See And sew on … *(page 39) for how to make a zippered case.*

YOU WILL NEED

- a 30 cm x 40 cm (12 in. x 16 in.) piece of sturdy fabric
- a 25 cm (10 in.) strip of hook-and-loop closure such as Velcro
- a 25 cm x 6 cm (10 in. x 2 1/4 in.) strip of the same fabric
- your sewing kit (page 4)

1 Zigzag-stitch (page 12) around the rectangle of fabric.

2 With the fabric right side up, center and pin the loopy side of the Velcro along one end. (Velcro is difficult to pin because of its thickness, so don't use too many pins.) Starting close to the zigzagged edge, stitch the Velcro in place. Remove the pins as you sew. When you get to the end, leave the needle in the Velcro, pivot, stitch the end, pivot and stitch the other side and end.

3 Stitch the hook side of the Velcro onto the other end of the rectangle as you did in step 2.

4 With the right sides together, fold and pin the fabric strip for the handle in half along its length. Stitch it using a 0.5 cm (¼ in.) seam allowance. Remove the pins as you sew.

5 Fasten a safety pin to the seam allowance at one end of the strip. Thread it through the fabric tube to turn it right side out. Remove the pin.

6 Iron (page 5) the handle so that the seam is along one side and the handle lays flat. Stitch close to each edge. Zigzag-stitch (page 12) the ends of the handle.

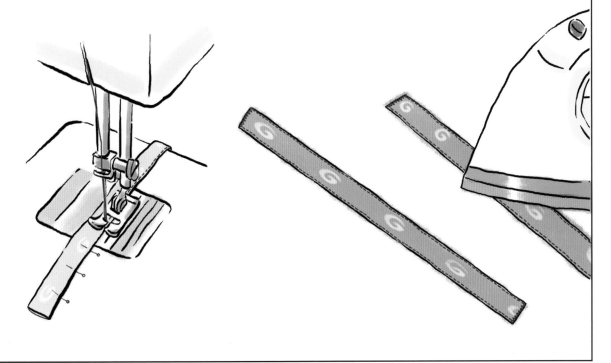

Instructions continue on the next page ☞

7 With the right sides together, fold the fabric for the bag in half so that the Velcro strips stick. Fold the handle in half and pin it between the layers of one side of the bag about 6 cm (2 ½ in.) from the top so that it is inside the bag. Pin the rest of the two sides together.

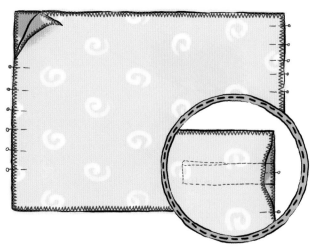

8 As you stitch the bag, sew back and forth a couple of times across the handle area to give it extra strength. Remove the pins as you sew.

9 Pull apart the Velcro. Fold over and pin the top of the bag the width of the Velcro. Following your Velcro stitching lines, sew around the top twice. Remove the pins as you sew.

10 Position the bottom corners as shown and stitch across them about 2.5 cm (1 in.) from each corner. Turn the bag right side out and fill it up!

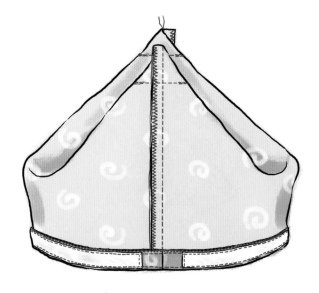

And sew on ...

⊙ For a zippered case, you'll need a 23 cm (9 in.) zipper and two 13 cm x 30 cm (6 in. x 12 in.) rectangles of fabric.

1. Zigzag-stitch around each rectangle. With the right sides together, pin the rectangles along one long edge.

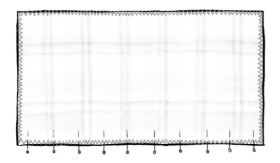

2. Follow steps 2 to 11 on pages 32 to 35 to put in a zipper.

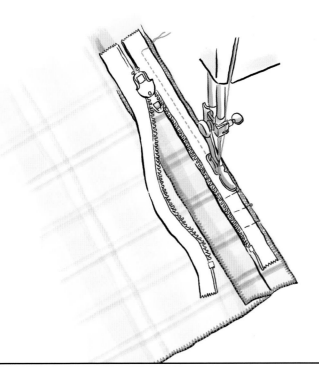

3. Change back to your regular machine's presser foot. Using a 1 cm (½ in.) seam allowance, pin and stitch the other three seams with the right sides together.

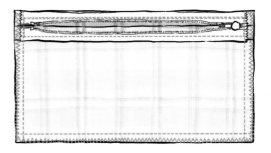

4. Turn it right side out. You may need to trim off some of the bulk in the corners. Use a short piece of ribbon, fancy trim or braided embroidery floss to thread through the hole in the zipper pull. Fold it in half and stitch or knot it in place. Apply nail polish or craft glue to the ends to keep them from fraying.

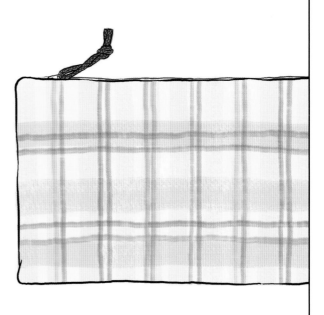

PJ pants

By tracing a pair of your own pants, you'll have a pattern that you can use to make cozy pajama pants, cool capris and bold boxers. Try flannelette for warmth, light cotton for summer and stretchy jersey-type fabrics for yoga and sporty wear.

YOU WILL NEED

- a large strip of plain newsprint or sheets of paper taped together
- a pair of pants in your size
- 2.5 m (2 ⅔ yds.) of fabric 115 cm (45 in.) wide or 1.5 m (1 ⅔ yds.) of fabric 150 cm (60 in.) wide, prewashed and ironed
- elastic 13 to 20 mm (½ to ¾ in.) wide (for length, see step 15)
- your sewing kit (page 4)

1 Lay the paper on a table or floor. Fold your pants in half by bringing the left side over the right and pulling the crotch area out to the left. Place the folded pants on the paper.

2 Trace closely around the pants. If they have a drawstring or elastic waist, make sure they are stretched out while you are tracing around the waist area. Set the pants aside.

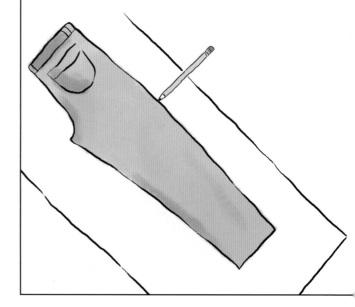

3 Draw the following lines outside of your traced lines: a 4 cm (1 ½ in.) line at the waist and bottom and a 2.5 cm (1 in.) line around the rest of the pants. Cut your paper pattern along the outside line.

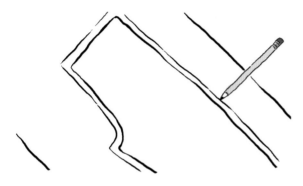

4 With the right sides together, fold the fabric along its length so that the widest point of the pattern fits across the folded fabric with very little extra fabric. Place the pattern's long, straight edge along the fabric fold and pin it in place.

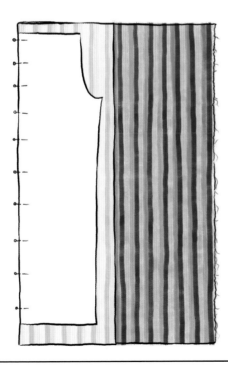

5 Cut around the pattern and remove the pins and pattern. Fold another area of the remaining fabric so that you can pin and cut out the pattern, again along the fabric fold.

6 Remove the pins and pattern. You should now have two identical fabric pattern pieces. With the right sides together and edges even, keep them folded and pin each one along the area from below the crotch to the bottom.

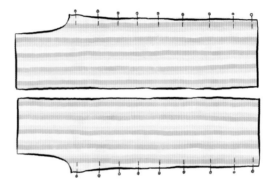

7 Stitch the pinned seams using a 1.5 cm (⅝ in.) seam allowance. Remove the pins as you sew.

8 Zigzag-stitch the four seam edges. Iron (page 5) the seams open. (Use a sleeve board if you have one.) These are the legs for your pants.

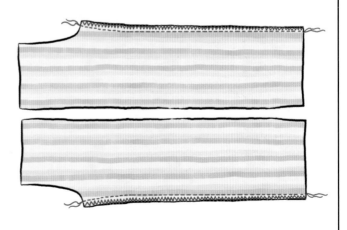

Instructions continue on the next page ☞

9 Turn one leg right side out. Tuck it inside the other leg and pin them as shown so that the seams are together and the rounded edges are even.

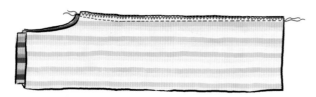

10 Stitch this seam using a 1.5 cm (⅝ in.) seam allowance. Stitch slowly around the curve. You may need to stop and, with the needle in the fabric, lift the presser foot so you can pivot to stay on the curve of the seam. Remove the pins as you sew.

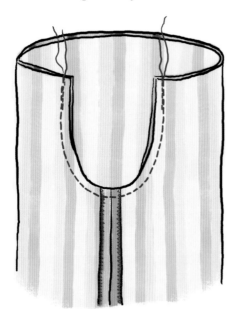

11 Stitch the seam again on top of your first stitch line to reinforce it. Trim the seam allowance to 0.5 cm (¼ in.) and zigzag-stitch the leftover seam edges together.

12 Pull the leg out of the other one, but keep the pants inside out. Zigzag-stitch around the top of the pants.

13 To make the casing for the elastic, fold over 1 cm (½ in.) to the wrong side around the zigzagged edge and iron it. Fold over, iron and pin an additional 2.5 cm (1 in.).

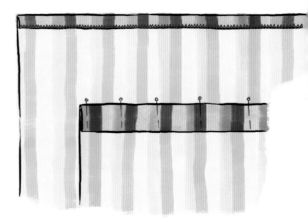

14 Starting at one seam, stitch the casing close to the inside edge. Stop stitching 4 cm (1 ½ in.) from where you started. Remove the pins as you sew.

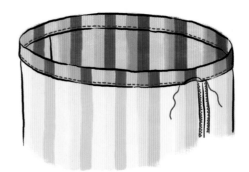

15 Measure around your waist, add 5 cm (2 in.) and cut the elastic to this length. Fasten a safety pin onto one end of the elastic and thread it through the casing.

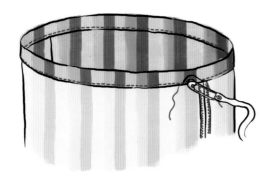

16 Overlap the elastic ends and safety-pin them together. Try on the pants to see if the elastic feels comfortable. Adjust it if necessary. Remove the pin and zigzag- or overcast-stitch (page 8) the elastic together.

17 Machine-stitch the opening closed.

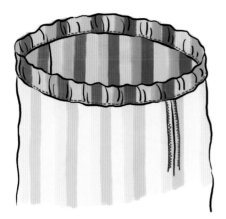

18 Fold over 1 cm (½ in.) to the wrong side around the hemline and iron it. Then fold over and iron an additional 2.5 cm (1 in.). Try on your pants. If they are too long, cut off some of the length then iron and pin up the hem. Stitch close to the inside edge. Remove the pins as you sew.

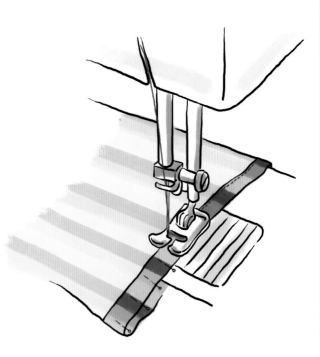

And sew on ...

To make capris, boxers or other short pj bottoms, cut off your paper pattern to the length you'd like your pajamas to be plus 3 cm (1 ¼ in.). (After you've cut out the fabric, tape the cut-off paper back onto the pattern.) Follow the instructions above to sew them together.

Machine appliqué

Machine appliqué is a great way to decorate your sewing projects. Use a fusible web such as Pellon Wonder-Under or HeatnBond Lite. These paper-backed, iron-on adhesives are available at fabric stores.

YOU WILL NEED

- fusible web   • small pieces of fabric
  - an item of clothing or a partially completed project from this book
  - your sewing kit (page 4) including thread to match your appliqué

Note: *Read the manufacturer's instructions on your fusible web in case they are different from the instructions below. Prewash and iron the item you will be appliquéing.*

1   Use a pencil to draw a shape directly onto the paper backing (the smooth side) of the fusible web. Or trace one of the patterns from pages 46 to 48 onto a sheet of paper, cut it out and trace it onto the back of the fusible web. The finished appliqué will be the reverse of your drawing or traced pattern.

2   Cut out your shape just outside of your pencil lines.

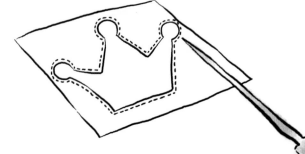

3 Place the shape, paper side up, onto the wrong side of a piece of fabric. Without steam and at a medium-high setting, iron (page 5) the shape for about 3 seconds.

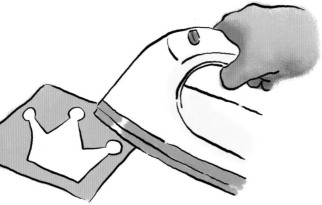

4 When the fabric is cool, cut out the shape along the pencil lines.

5 Remove the paper backing. Position the cutout, fabric side up (adhesive side down), on the right side of the clothing or fabric. Iron it for 5 to 7 seconds.

6 Set your sewing machine to zigzag (page 12) and adjust the stitch length so that the zigzag-stitches are narrow and close together. Make sure that as you slowly stitch around the edges of your cutout, the needle goes onto the appliqué shape on one stitch and just over the edge of the shape on the next stitch. Before you pivot, make sure the needle is in the fabric.

And sew on ...

● If you will be using the same fabric for many cutout shapes, cut a large piece of fusible web and iron it onto the wrong side of a slightly larger piece of fabric. Draw shapes onto it and cut them out along the pencil lines. Continue from step 4.

● After zigzagging your appliqué, you can stitch on buttons, beads or sequins or add details with dimensional fabric paint or embroidery floss.

Appliqué patterns

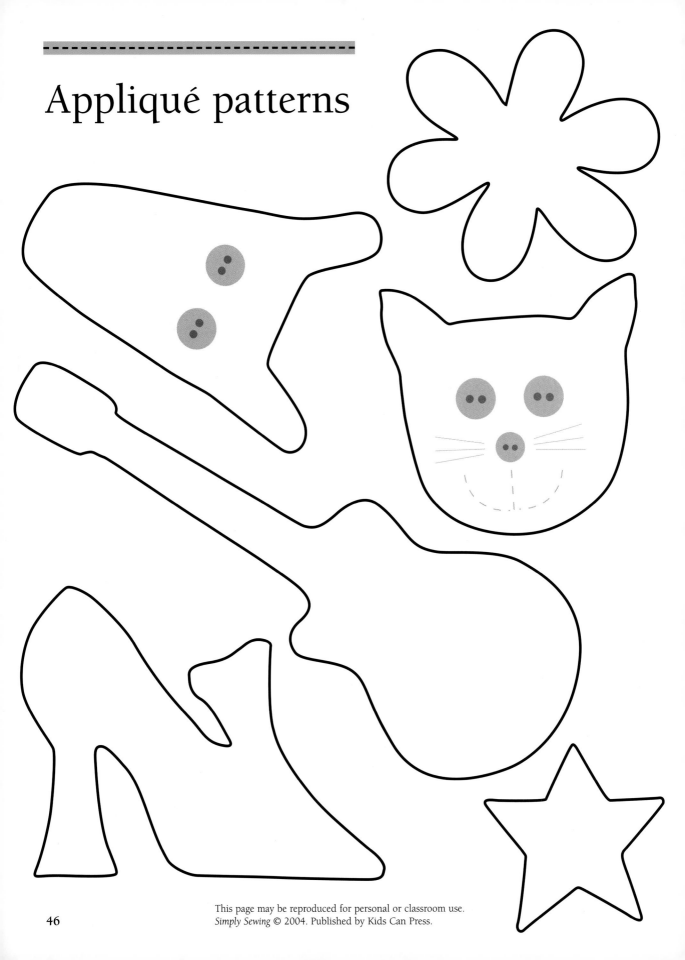